semiautomatic

semi

WESLEYAN UNIVERSITY PRESS

automatic

MIDDLETOWN, CONNECTICUT

evie
shockley

weleyan poetry

Wesleyan University Press

Middletown CT 06459

www.wesleyan.edu/wespress

2017 © Evie Shockley

All rights reserved

Manufactured in the United States of America

Designed by Quemadura

Typeset in DIN and Joanna

Untitled "Topsy" images by Alison Saar. Copyright © 2017

by Alison Saar. Used by permission of the artist.

Library of Congress Cataloging-in-Publication Data

Names: Shockley, Evie, 1965–, author

Title: Semiautomatic / Evie Shockley

Description: Middletown, Connecticut : Wesleyan University Press, 2017 | Series: Wesleyan Poetry

Identifiers: LCCN 2016059299 (print) | LCCN 2017006168 (ebook) | ISBN 9780819577436 (cloth : alk. paper) |
ISBN 9780819577443 (pbk. : alk. paper) | ISBN 9780819577450 (ebook)

Classification: LCC PS3619.H63 A6 2017 (print) | LCC PS3619.H63 (ebook) | DDC 811/.6—dc23

LC record available at https://lccn.loc.gov/2016059299

This project is supported in part by an award
from the National Endowment for the Arts

National
Endowment
for the Arts
arts.gov

5 4 3 2

for patrisse cullors, alicia garza, and opal tometi

movers of people, shakers of worlds

Have you ever suffered from political despair, from despair about the organization of things? What does it mean to suffer from political despair when your identity is bound up with utopian political aspirations and desires? How is identity reconfigured in the absence or betrayal of those aspirations? What's the relation between political despair and mourning?

—fred moten

are we not more than hunger and music?
are we not more than harlequins and horns?
are we not more than color and drums?
are we not more than anger and dance?

give me courage so i can spread it
over my face and mouth.

—sonia sanchez

As a culture worker who belongs to an oppressed people my job is to make revolution irresistible.

—toni cade bambara

contents

iii. refrain

iv. blues modality

Most discussions about 21st century political issues seemed to be constrained to academic settings

semiautomatic

that's a rap (sheet music for alphabet street)

if i sang the blues would that be new ? or knew ? would boos follow blues ? would blood follow, bud, flower, flow, sang-froid, cold-blooded, hot-blooded, male :: if i sang frigid would that be cool ? jazzy ? jizz, buzz, the word :: do i have the rite to write the body ? the right body to remain silent ? *habeas corpus*, to have the remains *dans mes mains*, my main man, handy man, unhand me, uncuff me, so i can speak in my sign(ifying) language :: signs, wonders, miracles, temptations :: three or four, tops :: hip hops, micro-brouhahas, address 'em and drop the mic :: ain't nothing new, son, about us being under the gun :: checked in the black box, never a dull minute, o pen it, mighty muse, flighty music, *put de light letters together*, take it away . . .

i.

o the times

I learn from the past
of others' mistakes.

—erica hunt

weather or not

time was on its side, its upside down. it was a new error. generation why-not had voted its con-science and a climate of indifference was generating maelstromy weather. we acted as if the planet was a stone-cold player, but turns out the earth had a heart and it was melting, pacific islanders first into the hotter water. just a coincidence—the polar bears are white and their real estate was being liquidated too. meanwhile, in the temper-temper zone, the birds were back and i hadn't slept—had it been a night or a season? the birdsong sounded cheap, my thoughts cheaper, penny, inky, dark. language struck me as wooden, battered. the words became weeds, meaning i couldn't see any use for them. i had signed my name repeatedly without any sign of change. i was still bleeding from yesterday's sound bites, and the coming elections were breeding candid hates by the hand-over-fistful. there'd been an arab spring, but it was winter all summer in america.

the way we live now ::

when the cultivators of corpses are busy seeding
plague across vast acres of the land, choking schools
    and churches in the motley toxins of grief, breeding
virile shoots of violence so soon verdant even fools
    fear to tread in their wake :: when all known tools
of resistance are clutched in the hands of the vile
    like a wilting bouquet, cut from their roots, while

the disempowered slice smiles across their own faces
    and hide the wet knives in writhing thickets of hair
for future use :: when breathing in the ashen traces
    of dreams deferred, the detonator's ticking a queer
echo that amplifies instead of fading :: when there-
    you-are is where-you-were and the sunset groans
into the atlantic, setting blue fire to dark white bones.

buried truths

self-evident [handwritten]

≈≈
≈≈
≈≈
≈≈
≈≈
≈≈

≈≈ are you not the sweet to rave on ≈ are you not the cold drama do- ≈≈
≈≈ and on about, the smart in ≈ ing hot duty, the remedy aloe ≈≈
≈≈ the sore, the phantasy so near, ≈ salving new york city's forty-one ≈≈
≈≈ so far from dark disney's phantom? ≈ gaping pus-filled wounds? ≈≈

≈≈
≈≈

≈≈ are you not the river jordan ≈ are you not the crimson mark ≈≈
≈≈ we must cross this very day, vis- ≈ circling the crater white brits dug in ≈≈
≈≈ ceral evidence of florida's abyss? ≈ the brown earth of tottenham? ≈≈

≈≈
≈≈

≈≈ are you not the handfuls of rice ≈ are you not the filamentary niche, a ≈≈
≈≈ thrown up in cleveland's tame air, ≈ sign of how fear will make bride ≈≈
≈≈ a cloud raining sharply down ≈ of blood, how it motors cities, ≈≈
≈≈ that will not be swept away? ≈ flaming, right off the map? ≈≈

≈≈
≈≈

≈≈ are you not the silvery key, a ≈ are you not the atmospheric ≈≈
≈≈ raft rigged with new vines, buoyed ≈ rush to infuse lungs dying to garner ≈≈
≈≈ by bronzeville's kitchenette arias? ≈ inspiring staten island breezes? ≈≈

≈≈
≈≈

≈≈ are you not the fertile mystery ca- ≈ are you not the jet stream germane ≈≈
≈≈ joling hope, despite narrow ills, on ≈ to the question of whose scar be- ≈≈
≈≈ a half-plucked wing and a half-heard ≈ comes whose scare, screams or tires ≈≈
≈≈ prayer in lima, ohio's wasted land? ≈ peeling on greater toronto streets? ≈≈

≈≈
≈≈

≈≈ are you not the music's ignition, ≈ are you not the young life ready ≈≈
≈≈ the beat, the bass, and the bell ≈ to explode from the wet shell of gray ≈≈
≈≈ sounding new york's belated alarm? ≈ into riotous mobtown flower? ≈≈

≈≈
≈≈
≈≈≈≈≈≈≈≈≈≈≈≈≈≈≈≈≈≈≈≈≈≈≈≈≈≈≈≈≈≈≈≈≈ —*after keorapetse kgositsile* ≈
≈≈

what's not to liken?

the 14-year-old girl was treated like:

    (a) a grown woman.

    (b) a grown man.

the bikini-clad girl was handled by the cop like:

    (a) a prostitute.

    (b) a prostitute by her pimp.

the girl was slung to the ground like:

    (a) a sack of garbage into a dumpster.

    (b) somebody had something to prove.

the girl's braids flew around her head like:

    (a) helicopter blades.

    (b) she'd been slapped.

the black girl was pinned to the ground like:

    (a) an amateur wrestler in a professional fight.

    (b) swimming in a private pool is a threat to national security.

the girl's cries sounded like:

    (a) the shrieks of children on a playground.

    (b) the shrieks of children being torn from their mothers.

the protesting girl was shackled like:

    (a) a criminal.

    (b) a runaway slave.

liken it or not

even if they aren't related or shouldn't be

—mckinney, texas, june 2015

playing with fire

something is always burning, passion,
               pride, envy, desire, the internal organs
     going chokingly up in smoke, as some-
          thing outside the body exerts a pull
that drags us like a match across sand-
             paper. something is always burning,
london, paris, detroit, l.a., the neighbor-

          hoods no one outside seems to see until
they're backlit by flames: then the out-
          siders, peering through dense, acrid,
     black-&-orange-rimmed fumes, mis-
          take their dark reflections for savages
altogether alien. how hot are the london
             riots for west end pearls? how hot in tot-

tenham? black blood's highly combustible,
          under conditions of sufficient pressure—
measured roughly in years + lead ÷ £s.
          but if one bead of cream rolls down one
     precious neck, heads will roll in brix-
          ton. the science of sociology. the mark
duggan principle of cause and effect.

mirror and canvas

self-portrait with cats, with purple, with stacks
    of half-read books adorning my desk, with coffee,

        with mug, with yesterday's mug. self-portrait
    with guilt, with fear, with thick-banded silver ring,

    painted toes, and no make-up on my face. self-
        portrait with twins, with giggles, with sister at

        last, with epistrophy, with crepuscule with nellie,
with my favorite things. self-portrait with hard

head, with soft light, with raised eyebrow. self-
    portrait voodoo, self-portrait hijinks, self-portrait

        surprise. self-portrait with patience, with political
    protest, with poetry, with papers to grade. self-

portrait as thaumaturgic lass, self-portrait as luna
    larva, self-portrait as your mama. self-portrait

        with self at sixteen. self-portrait with shit-kickers,
with hip-huggers, with crimson silk, with wild

mushroom risotto and a glass of malbec. self-
    portrait with partial disclosure, self-portrait with

half-truths, self-portrait with demi-monde. self-
portrait with a night at the beach, with a view

overlooking the lake, with cancelled flight. self-
portrait with a real future, with a slight chance of

sours, with glasses, with cream, with fries, with
a way with words, with a propositional phrase.

if a junco

~ a vocabulary takes us under its wing ~ a vestibule soft until ruffled ~ it muffles our voices with its muscles and down ~ do we pluck it bare ~ then what of flight ~ a lexicon connives against us when we are busy admiring its plumage ~ does the music of its mating call seduce ~ if we crack its hollow bones and blow ~ will such broken notes carry ~ us ~ how far ~ a language spreads its tail ~ draws our eyes to its outer feathers flashing white ~ when it snaps shut the fan ~ will we lose sight of what we are saying ~ can we fly blind ~ can we fly right ~ can we fly-by-night ~ see ~ already ~ what are we whistling ~

banking on amnesia (*america*)

manhattan was preoccupied with the price of beads.

chicago, illinois, was preoccupied with du sable's black fur trade.

tennessee was preoccupied with following the market in lachrymal saline :: it had
        been trailing since jackson was in office.

massachusetts was preoccupied with the steep cost of religious pilgrimage.

tulsa, oklahoma, was preoccupied with one kind of black gold :: it didn't place
        much stock in the other kind.

alaska was preoccupied first with the rush on fur, then with the mining industry.

the dakotas were preoccupied with wheat as a cash crop ;: they were railroaded
        into it.

minnesota was preoccupied with timber, which was grist for the mill.

texas was preoccupied with first one thing then another :: its economy flagged
        until oil surfaced.

missouri was preoccupied with the louisiana purchase.

arizona was preoccupied with a bankrupt christianizing mission :: it went from
        broke to broker.

alabama was preoccupied with agriculture from the start, other futures foreclosed until it acquired a coastline.

mississippi, was preoccupied with blankets and bullets, incorporating them into its culture in exchange for mounds and mounds of land.

a one-act play

lights up on 3 people, unmoving. not all of them are the same gender. none of them are touching. each of them is looking at another. the moon is full. the stock market is down. the ball is rolling. all bets are off. we hear a loud noise: a gunshot. a scream. a burst of thunderous applause. it comes from off-stage. on-stage, all 3 hear the noise as a signal to act. the moment each begins to act, the lights go down. when they come back up, just seconds later, everything has changed. it has something to do with race, but it's debatable how much. it's something that somebody said, but it's not clear who, if anyone, heard. it's about a million acts, but we'll all play like it was just one. each person has lines to give. anyone who knows it can write the script.

in a no-win zone

we remain ever in six x six rooms, on ice, unseen :
we consume no sun or moon views : we sew our
concise seam, same as ever : we receive no new air,
never roam, never run across a wren, a sure omen :
we once were warriors : now our sorrows rain on
us : our rosier news is no nooses : we mourn ruinous
memories, mine rue, see no surcease : woe is we :
some insane sin or crass crime means we weave our
remorse in an iron maze, women, men in an ominous
zoo : we seem mean so we can survive, a zero sum, no
score, or worse, we owe : nervous, we are unsure our
voices can save us : we scream, more room now : we
vow, no more war : our vices over, we are sore users :
wave au revoir : soon we resume our ravenous music

corrective rape (or, i'm here to help)

—for millicent gaika and all the sisters getting "rescued" from our own beautiful selves

(*the doctor's advice:*)

you won't know it's you in the mirror : it'll make you normal : you won't stick out like a black eye : think of it as a kind of *out-patient surgery* : you'll be more like god intended : expect to require a brief recovery period : you deserve this : it gets rid of irregularities : you'll be right as reined : this procedure may hurt a little : you'll feel so much better about yourself : i'll fix it so you come correct

Sex Trafficking Incidents in the

Life of a Slave Girl in the USA

(or, The Nation's Plague in Plain Sight)

And now, reader, I come to a period in my unhappy life, which I would gladly forget if I could. *Asia Graves looks straight ahead as she calmly recalls the night a man paid $200 on a Boston street to have sex with her.*

The remembrance fills me with sorrow and shame. *"If you want attention and you see that you're getting it, you just follow your feelings," senior Araceli Figueroa, 17, said. "It's sad."*

It pains me to tell you of it; but I have promised to tell you the truth, and I will do it honestly, let it cost me what it may. *A plague more commonly associated with other countries has been taking young victims in the United States, one by one.*

I will not try to screen myself behind the plea of compulsion from a master; for it was not so. *"They give you money, drugs and a fun time, but in the end they want your dignity and your self-respect," she said. "It's invisible chains that these kids are tied with."*

Neither can I plead ignorance or thoughtlessness. By day,
she was a school girl who saw her family occasionally.

For years, my master had done his utmost to pollute my
mind with foul images, and to destroy the pure principles
inculcated by my grandmother, and the good mistress of
my childhood. *The [outreach] efforts by high school and middle-
school officials in Washington, D.C., Virginia, Connecticut, Oregon,
Wisconsin, California and Florida come as experts say criminals
have turned to classrooms and social media sites to recruit students
into forced domestic sex and labor rings.*

The influences of slavery had had the same effect on me
that they had on other young girls; they had made me pre-
maturely knowing, concerning the evil ways of the world.
*Sold from Boston to Miami and back, Graves was one of thousands
of young girls sexually exploited across the United States, often in
plain sight.*

*Though the scope of the problem remains uncertain—no national statistics for
the number of U.S. victims exist—the National Center for Missing and Ex-
ploited Children says at least 100,000 children across the country are traf-
ficked each year. Globally, the International Labor Organization estimates
that about 20.9 million people are trafficked and that 22% of them are victims
of forced sexual exploitation.*

I knew what I did, and I did it with deliberate calculation. *From ages 14 to 17, [Katariina Rosenblatt] says she was drugged, abused, raped and trafficked by several people including [a class-mate's] father's friends, a neighbor who ran a trafficking house, and man who offered her a role in a movie.*

But, O, ye happy women, whose purity has been sheltered from childhood, who have been free to choose the objects of your affection, whose homes are protected by law, do not judge the poor desolate slave girl too severely! *"I want to raise the compassion bar so that any girl who becomes a victim is never seen as a girl who asked for it,"* said Andrea Powell, executive director of Fair Girls.

Among others, it chanced that a white unmarried gentleman had obtained some knowledge of the circumstances in which I was placed. He knew my grandmother, and often spoke to me in the street. *The perpetrators—increasingly younger—can be other students or gang members who manipulate victims' weaknesses during recess or after school, law enforcement officials say.*

He became interested for me, and asked questions about my master, which I answered in part. He expressed a great deal of sympathy, and a wish to aid me. *At night, she became a slave to men who said they loved her and convinced her to trade her beauty for quick cash that they pocketed.*

He constantly sought opportunities to see me, and wrote to me frequently. *They often bait victims by telling them they will be beautiful strippers or escorts but later ply them with drugs—ecstasy pills, cocaine, marijuana and the like—and force them into sex schemes.*

I was a poor slave girl, only fifteen years old. *She was 16, homeless, and desperate for food, shelter and stability.*

So much attention from a superior person was, of course, flattering; for human nature is the same in all. *She was alone on a corner in Boston during a snowstorm when her first trafficker picked her up.*

I also felt grateful for his sympathy, and encouraged by his kind words. *Young people at the fringes of school, runaways looking for someone to care and previously abused victims fall into the traps of traffickers who often pretend to love them.*

It seemed to me a great thing to have such a friend. *"He said I was too pretty to stay outside, so I ended up going home with him because he offered me a place to sleep and clothes to put on," she said.*

By degrees, a more tender feeling crept into my heart. *"It's about love and thinking you're part of a family and a team."*

He was an educated and eloquent gentleman; too eloquent, alas, for the poor slave girl who trusted in him. "*When a little girl is sold by her impoverished family, or girls my daughters' ages run away from home and are lured—that's slavery,*" [President] Obama said. "*It's barbaric, it's evil, and it has no place in a civilized world.*"

Of course I saw whither all this was tending. *The man said he wanted to take care of her but that she would have to earn her keep.* "*He showed me the ropes,*" *she said.* "*How much to charge for sex*" *and other sex acts.*

I knew the impassable gulf between us; but to be an object of interest to a man who is not married, and who is not her master, is agreeable to the pride and feelings of a slave, if her miserable situation has left her any pride or sentiment.

It seems less degrading to give one's self, than to submit to compulsion. *She stayed, however, and found comfort in other girls—called "wife in-laws"—who went to area schools, got their hair and nails done together and then worked the streets for the same man.*

There is something akin to freedom in having a lover who has no control over you, except that which he gains by kindness and attachment. *Then came the violence. Her attempts to leave were met with brute force.* "*He punched me. He stripped me down naked and beat me.*"

A master may treat you as rudely as he pleases, and you dare not speak; moreover, the wrong does not seem so great with an unmarried man, as with one who has a wife to be made unhappy. *Other violent episodes left her with eight broken teeth, two broken ankles and a V-shaped stab wound just below her belly button.*

There may be sophistry in all this; but the condition of a slave confuses all principles of morality, and, in fact, renders the practice of them impossible. *"You think what you're doing is right when you're in that lifestyle," Graves said. "You drink alcohol to ease the stress. Red Bulls kept you awake, and cigarettes kept you from being hungry."*

I was sure my friend, Mr. Sands, would buy me. *For two years, she was sold from tormentor to tormentor, forced to sleep with men in cities like New York, Atlanta, Philadelphia, Atlantic City, Miami.*

He was a man of more generosity and feeling than my master, and I thought my freedom could be easily obtained from him. *"They said they were escorts and that they made $2,000 a night. I figured if I go out one night, I'll never have to do it again."*

"You can sell drugs once," says Alessandra Serano, an Assistant United States Attorney for the Southern District of California. "You can sell a girl thousands of times."

With all these thoughts revolving in my mind, and seeing no other way of escaping the doom I so much dreaded, I made a headlong plunge. *He was the first of dozens of men who would buy her thin cashew-colored body from a human trafficker who exploited her vulnerabilities and made her a prisoner for years.*

Pity me, and pardon me, O virtuous reader! *"They are as horrific and brutal and vile as any criminal cases we see," said Neil MacBride, the U.S. Attorney for the Eastern District of Virginia.*

You never knew what it is to be a slave; to be entirely unprotected by law or custom; to have the laws reduce you to the condition of a chattel, entirely subject to the will of another. *"I couldn't leave because I thought he would kill me."*

You never exhausted your ingenuity in avoiding the snares, and eluding the power of a hated tyrant; you never shuddered at the sound of his footsteps, and trembled within hearing of his voice. *"If we didn't call him daddy, he would slap us, beat us, choke us," said Graves of the man who organized the deals.*

I know I did wrong. No one can feel it more sensibly than I do. The painful and humiliating memory will haunt me to my dying day. *One girl was sold during a sleepover, handed over by her classmate's father. Another slept with clients during her school lunch breaks. A third was choked by her "boyfriend," then forced to have sex with 14 men in one night.*

Still, in looking back, calmly, on the events of my life, I feel that the slave woman ought not to be judged by the same standard as others. *For some of the time, Graves herself remained in high school, attending classes sporadically in boy shorts, small tank tops and worn heels. "In the schools, they thought I just dressed provocatively," Graves said of the teachers and staff who missed chances to help her. "Now, people are actually understanding that these girls are victims."*

What could I do? I thought and thought, till I became desperate, and made a plunge into the abyss.

ii.

the
topsy
suite

A young black girl stopped by the woods,
so young she knew only one man: Jim Crow
but she wasn't allowed to call him Mister.
   . . .

Of course she delighted in the filling up
of his woods, she so accustomed to emptiness,
to being taken at face value.

                         —thylias moss

studies in antebellum literature

(or, topsy-turvy)

19th-century novels paint
quite the chromatic picture

of america—take the white
whale, say, or the scarlet

letter—but they aren't
all tarred with the same

brush. for comic contrast
some give us black humor:

national relief projected
onto one dark little head,

in turn projecting, in all
directions, a local choler.

#   #   #

antebellum lit still tinges
tongues with shady tints.

our language is loaded,
packing heat, a weapon

concealed only, it seems,
from the blissful. who'd

say x used to be a small
college town, but then ten

years ago it just grew like
topsy? i'd say it grew like

kudzu, maybe. or like
wildfire. not like topsy.*

* things that just grew
like topsy: the middle

passage death toll.
the black prison

population. the crop
of negro spirituals. like

crazy. like a weed. like
a motherless child.

topsy's notes on taxonomy

your thumbs may be opposable (i'm opposed
to being under them) ~ and your communication
    may be complex (colored, coded) ~ but the closer

the ocean gets to cauldron, the more specious
    your classification be ~ if you love your specie
more than your species ~ you're out of order ~

        the darwinian emphasis on descent is quaint,
      but perhaps he's not acquainted with the finer
        distinctions of nineteenth-century science ~ see,

    i'm my master's flesh and blood ~ he tends
        to me, to them, as if they were his own (raw-

    hide, quick kiss, intimate, hit it), as tenderly
        as if i were legal tender ~ but pound for pound,
he'd never take the likes of me for human ~

    o believe me, whippersnapper, i'm whip-
smarter than i look ~ linnaeus' system made
    some sense ~ shared characteristics matter ~

let me put it to you plain ~ if i can't tell
    the difference between you and kudzu, it ain't
'cause my plaits're too tight ~ look at how

    y'all do ~ invade a foreign territory ~ no
invitation, no departure date ~ and jes'
    grow ~ Man o Man, you're not my kind ~

topsy talks about her role

i don't mean to get into their heads—i
jes' go. it's like i'm possessed, too: as if

my mind and body aren't my own. any-
how, it's all in the timing. if i desert a girl

too soon, she'll end up thirty before she's
thirteen, dragging around a burden big

as a church at an age when some young
women ain't weighing nothing heavier

than which purple they want for their
pedicure. but if i hold a sister too long,

not a thing on earth can tether her. now,
this sandra was anything but bland. i

was hooked! i do like to ride a tongue
that's limber, that can keep up with

the flash of my spirit. she had a dancing
mouth, the kind that could give you

warm—such warmth!—or just as easily
give you hot, if called for. i know where

i'm welcome. i was still cutting capers
behind her smile the week she died. i

overstayed. in texas—parts of chicago,
too—pickaninny-droll don't come in

women's sizes. you can set whatever
tone you want with a pair of baby-blues.

but when i roll black women's brown
eyes, they always turn into sapphires.

—for sandra bland (1987–2015)

from *topsy in wonderland*

what are you? said the captain of industry. this was not an encouraging opening for a conversation. topsy replied, gaily, <i hardly knows, suh, presently. i knowed who i was when i got up on my own continent this morning, but,> looks around the plantustation and the rest of the united states, <i musta been changed sev'ral times since then!>

a.i.w., ch. 5

<how'm i gonna get in?> asked topsy in a loud tone (presumably the only one she had). are you to get in at all? said the gatekeeper. that's the first question, you know. it was, no doubt: only topsy did not like to be told so.

a.i.w., ch. 6

yours wasn't a really good school, said the mocking person. *i took the different branches of arithmetic— ambition, distraction, uglification, and derision.* <i never did hear of 'uglification,'> topsy ventured to say. <what that be?> never heard of ugli-fying! he exclaimed. *you know what to beautify is, i suppose?* <yeah,> said topsy doubtfully: <it mean—to—make—somethin'— whiter.> well, then, the mocking person went on, if you don't know what to uglify is, you are a savage.

a.i.w., ch. 9

one thing was certain, that the *white* girl had had nothing to do with it—it was the black girl's fault entirely. for little eva had been having her sins washed away for the last three or four hundred years (and having begun as an apple-tart thief, thou-sands of years back, she was cleaning up pretty well, considering): so you see that she *couldn't* have had any hand in any contemporary mischief.

t.t.l., ch. 1

i should experience freedom far better, said topsy to herself, *if i could get to the mountaintop: and here's a path that leads directly to it—at least, no, it doesn't do that*—(after going a few yards along the path, and turning several sharp corners), *but i suppose it will get me free at last. but how curiously it twists! it's more like gerrymandering than meandering! well, this turn goes to the mountaintop, i suppose—no, it doesn't! this goes directly back to the big house! well then, i'll try another way.*

and so she did: wandering up and down, and trying tactic after tactic, but always coming back to the big house, do what she would. indeed, once, when topsy turned a corner rather more quickly than usual, she ran against it before she could stop herself. *i'm not going in again. i know i should have to go back through the looking-glass— back into the old box— and there'd be an end of all my efforts to escape!*

so, resolutely turning her back upon the big house, topsy set out once more through the system, determined to keep right on till she got to the mountaintop. for a few years all went on well, and she was just saying *i really shall do it this time*— when the path gave a sudden twist and the system shook itself, and the next moment she found herself actually walking in through the big house door.

oh, fuck the bullshit! topsy cried. *i never saw such a house for getting in the way! never!* however, there was the mountaintop full in sight, so there was nothing to be done but start again.

t.t.l., ch. 2

<lawsy, i sho wish i was a player in this here game! i wouldn't mind bein a pawn, if only i could join— *course i'd sho'nuff like to be a queen.*> her companion only smiled pleasantly, and said *that's easily managed. you can be the white queen's pawn, if you like; you're in square one to begin with: when you get to the eighth square you'll a queen be.*

t.t.l., ch. 2

just at this moment, they began to run. all topsy remembers is they were running, hand in hand, so fast that it was all she could do to keep up, and still the word was *faster! faster!* but she felt she *could not* go faster, though she had no breath left to say so. suddenly, just as topsy was getting quite exhausted, they stopped, and she found herself sitting on the ground, breathless and dizzy. topsy looked round her in great surprise. <*lawd, i do believe we been under this here foot the whole time! everythin's jes' as it was!*> *of course it is,* said the queen. *how would you have it?* <*well, back in my country,*> said topsy, still panting a little, <*you'd gen'rally get somewhere else— if you ran real fast for a long time like we been doin.*> *a slow sort of country!* said the queen. *now, here, you see, it takes all the running you can do, to keep in the same place. if you want to get somewhere else, you must run at least twice as fast as that.*

t.t.l., ch. 2

<*is i addressin the missus?*> topsy began. *well, yes, if you call that a-dressing,* the mistress said. *it isn't my notion of the thing, at all. i've been a-dressing myself for the last two hours.* it would have been all the better, it seemed to topsy, if she had got some one else to dress her, she was so dreadfully untidy and crooked. <*missus, you really seems to need*

a maid!> i'm sure i'll take you with pleasure! the mistress said. *two hundred hours a week, and freedom every other day.* topsy laughed nervously. <i don't want you to take me— i want my freedom to-day.> *you can't have it just because you want it,* the mistress said. *the rule is, freedom to-morrow and freedom yesterday— but never freedom to-day.* topsy objected. <it got to come sometime to 'freedom now!'>

t.t.l., ch. 5

now, reader, let's consider who dreamed it all . . .

iii.

refrain

From the first it had been like a

Ballad. It had the beat inevitable. It had the blood.

—gwendolyn brooks

a-lyrical ballad (or, how america

reminds us of the value of family)

he was a boy from chicago, in mississippi heat,
being as bad as a good boy could be,
whistling his eyeful of an off-limits she,

    and her menfolk dragged him out of bed, beat him to death, tied
    a cotton gin to his body, and sank him in the tallahatchie river.

it was three days before the remains were retrieved.
and the family grieved ~ o ~ the black family grieved

she was a lively young woman, a texas transplant,
with a new job helping black college kids thrive,
daring one day to assert her right to drive,

    and for failing to give a signal, a cop slammed her head down, <u>cheered</u>
    for her epilepsy, and dragged her to a cell where she died in three days.

they called it ~~suicide~~ *silence* if that can be conceived.
and the family grieved ~ o ~ the black family grieved

usually framed in this manner
he was a guinean emigrant, two years in new york,
a hard-working man, religiously devout,
<u>who reached in a pocket to take his id out,</u> *no trust*

    when 4 officers, suspecting (wrongly) that he was armed, unloaded their
    9-millimeter <u>semiautomatic</u> pistols into his body (<u>41 shots, just to be safe</u>),

to learn that he wasn't the threat they'd believed.
and the family grieved ~ o ~ the black family grieved

a fun-loving teen, having car trouble one night,
still seeking help when her cell phone died,
knocked on a nearby door, but the man inside

    barely took a look at the black person on his porch, before
    he shot her, point blank, through the closed screen door.

in this way his unfounded fears were relieved.
and the family grieved ~ o ~ the black family grieved

he was a sweet-toothed teen under florida sun,
just sipping iced tea, chatting on the phone,
but a local vigilante wouldn't leave him alone,

    and even after 911 instructed him to leave it for the police to handle,
    pulled a gun, started a fight, then legally—lethally—stood his ground.

and, yes, "self-defense" was how this was perceived.
and the family grieved ~ o ~ the black family grieved

she was a vibrant young woman, hanging in the park,
enjoying outdoors, chillin with her crew,
making some noise as good times often do,

    when an off-duty cop, mad that they refused to get quiet and worried
    that someone's phone was a gun, shot from his car into the crowd,

and the young woman's death was all he achieved.
and the family grieved ~ o ~ the black family grieved

he was a black kid playing in a cleveland park,
not the first or last boy to have a toy gun.
just goofing off, not pointing it *at* anyone,

    and the rookie cop, responding to a caller concerned that the kid *might*
    have a real weapon, arrived and, in 11 seconds flat, shot him dead . . .

. . . and the story goes on: the privileged are aggrieved,
or their eyes are "deceived,"
and another family's bereaved ~ o ~ the black family be grieved

keep your eye on

michael brown's body has a hole in it(   )
michael brown's murder has a hole in it(   )
michael brown's news coverage has a hole in it(   )
and they stopped it up with (   )

A HOT MESS™ IS MORE   important
                        likely   THAN A HOT BREAKFAST!
                        effective

(shoulda let them panthers do they thing . . .)

through the holes in michael brown's body,   i see:
- ▶ the fucking fracking chemicals bleeding into the groundwater
- ▶ the oilfields of northern africa and the lithium mines of afghanistan
- ▶ the flood of black and brown people seeping between prison bars
- ▶ the coke brothers controlling the flow

through the holes in michael brown's murder,   i see:
- ▶ the GMO CEO of monsanto
- ▶ the gazans stripped of dignity property
- ▶ the wrecking ball slamming like an afterthought through p.s. 1 – p.s. 1 million
- ▶ the supreme kangarulings that court corporate dollars

through the holes in michael brown's news coverage,   i see:
- ▶ the ███ hovering overhead in an amazonian cloud near you
- ▶ the fight for beyoncé's soul and george clooney's wedding photos
- ▶ the iraqi dead and the silence of all the lambs, including the black sheep
- ▶ the most civil disobedience money can buy

wave your hands up in the air

     waive your rights like you just don't care

         FCC is for cookies, that's good enough for me

          sprawl-mart employees can:

             (a) buy their own uniforms

             (b) afford their own uniforms

             (c) buy **from sprawl-mart**—at everyday low prices—the vests

                   that meet the new **sprawl-mart dress code** (because

                   uniforms must be supplied by the employer)

    [i . . . (c)? si!]

    john brown's ford(ism) has a hole in its tire . . . chew on that

                                        .

[where is this poem going???   black to the future!!!

                             off the rails!!!

                             to hell in a handbasket!!!

                             where no woman has gone before!!!]

   mine eyes have seen the orgy of the launching of the sword

   mine eyes have seen the fury of the protected and served

   mine eyes have seen the stories that are hidden and ignored

   mine eyes have seen

   mine eyes

                    (whose

                         truth

                              is

                                   mar

                                        ching

                                             on . . .

reading this reminds me of the overwhelming feeling I recieve when reading the news

DOW JONES 10/14/2014: SYRIAN REFUGEES UP TO 200,000 . . . SYRIAN
DEAD UP 500 "MOSTLY" FIGHTERS . . . YOU CAN SKIP THIS AD AFTER 5
SECONDS: EBOLA! EBOLA! EBOLA! EBOLA! EBOLA! EBOLA! EBOLA! . . .
"CLIMATE CHANGE IS FOR THE BIRDS" TWEETS HIGH-RANKING SENATOR
. . . MICHELLE OBAMA'S STRIKING ARMS RAISE CONTROVERSY . . .
WILL MILEY CYRUS BECOME THE NEXT LINDSAY LOHAN OR THE NEXT
MICHAEL JACKSON? . . . 30-FOOT FENCE AROUND U.S. BORDERS CAN'T
STOP ILLEGAL ALIENS; LITTLE GREEN MAN TELLS "HOW I GOT OVAH" . . .

          i see london
               princessfdiuwouldkbeuproudsofhanti-bullyingicharity,msayasons
          i see france
               parisahostsiafricanrdesignerssintweirdrseparatei"blackkfashionweek"
air strike i see uncle sam's underpants
               trayvonimartinmjordanpdaviserenisharmcbrideimichaelabrownlism . . .

                              the arabic word for freedom is on fire!
                              the french word for freedom was torched!
                              the american word for freedom was exported!

48

(when a bloody shame dies, hope gets in your eyes)
(i can see clearer now, the gain is gone)
(the body is real, but tears blur the vision)

i see   *the ball*

i see   *the money*

i see   *the grand old flag*   ♪

haibun for a parasitic pre-apocalyptic blues

on the nature walk at tahoe, i learned everything the secret life of flora could teach me about creatures that don't know what to do with light besides admire and squander it :: for instance, the snow plant is not white, but sings the humming-birds its red siren song as soon as the snow recedes in spring :: it wears no green slip or wrap :: crimson from stem to stern, this barely-plant skips photosynthesis, stalks pines, and steals sugar from their mycorrhizal web :: (trickle-down symbio-sis is no symbiosis at all) :: in their language, the washoe called this squat, blunt, scarlet getter _coyote penis_ :: it doesn't just _look_ like a dick—

> a small flame
> burns the snows away—
> keeps your eye off the subterranean subterfuge

sore score

ugly :: no, nothing more than a scab :: a pain(t)ob, applied
biology, wound-be-gone, but meanwhile :: black-brown
patch :: skin-music, band-aid, home-grown :: (stuck) :: itching
to beat the band, itching to disappear, magic foiled, the urge
to peek piqued :: (picked): well enough not let alone :: pink
the price to pay :: raw news, read meat, rough cut :: (edit)

description at the press new the us. war on communities of color

similar to the title page

red to black like a scab

in the california mountains, far from shelby

county, alabama, and even farther from

     the supreme court building, the black poet

seeks the low-down from a kindred entity

seep-spring monkey flower, growing
     up from the scorched earth of last
year's planned burn: looks like you,
      too, know how to get what you need

     under cover of darkness. sunshine's
only half the story. when light becomes
     fire, we reach down and let our roots
sustain us till the topsoil's ready for

our comeback. we're all aware there's
     no justice in drought: and whoever
says this weather's nobody's fault has
     just bought a bridge they hope to resell.

     like you, we're perennial in warmer
climes. we've also been called monkey,
     and didn't get to vote on that either.
so: can we pay a poll tax with pollen?

i declare war

high-stakes cards. three

up. nine beats five. queen

resource-rich land. cards

collateral damage. kings

wilder. it used to take two

to commit this country

now it only takes one joker

of diamonds takes wells

takes port au prince. four's

talking. i. *de. clare. war.* in

in a game where we risk

chief seeks popular, not

he holds his cards close

and on about how smart

his deck. he's a real player.

hidden, the fourth turned

beats ten. winner takes all

lying face down may hide

are wild, but presidents are

branches of government

to international conflict.

willing to pull rank. queen

of oil. jack of diamonds

met with four? we're done

seconds, we're involved

everything. our ace-in-

congressional, support.

to the chest. he drones on

his bombs are. how thick

you don't say. i do declare.

acrobatic

acrophiliac i'm not, so don't try putting me on the balance
beam. the rings, too, are a bad idea—it doesn't help having
chalk on my hands. it seems that when you think of me, you think
daredevil, some simone biles, but that's just ignorant. as
everybody else knows, i'm a close-to-the-mat
freestyler, just bouncing along to the music from *rocky*. you couldn't
get me as far off the ground as the uneven bars.
heights make my skin break out and my eyes
implode. since as far back as i can remember, i've avoided
jungle gyms—if god meant us to climb, he'd have given all
kindergarteners tails. you'll never catch me on a ski
lift, a ski slope, or a ski. there are just too
many ways to die, when you start fucking with altitude.
next, you'll be asking me to high dive. listen: i need my
oxygen. if i was any taller, i'd get dizzy
parting my hair. surely you know that mountains are—without
question—the greatest mistake mother nature made. give me one good
reason to ride a roller coaster. i don't even like mood
swings. you can keep the carnival—the flying
trapeze is an absolute no-go, even with a safety net
underneath. i start dragging my heels at the suggestion of the pole
vault—i'd never let go. i'll watch the fabulous janelle monae
walk the tightrope all day, but that's not my dance. i'm as
xenial as anyone, but my out-of-towners don't get tours of towers. my
yoga routine revolves around downward facing dog. really, not even
zeus in his swan suit could sweep me off my feet.

song in the back yard

—a golden shovel for rihanna

[handwritten: a depiction of black woman]

the more you see   the less you see me   <u>tattoos</u> and
thighs crowd your eyes   i'm young but i've seen scenes i'd
pay well to unwitness   plays as old as power   an ancient script   you like
my hair   my ass   my tits   if you had to
<u>sell my voice</u>   how would you package it   would it be
pretty in pink   with dancehall in my spit and a
childhood of training in denial   <u>mi make it *good girl gone bad*</u>
gone red   seen red   seen blue black scream-swollen song scene   woman
down   i didn't do it   *this was done to me*   and <u>*my love is too*</u>

<u>*complicated to have thrown back in my face*</u>   and
it's got nothing to do with the clothes i wear
he was my friend   he was my father   <u>i was my mother</u>   the
ancient script again   now casting a <u>new generation</u>   you got to be brave
when every minute of your day is a press / release   my stockings
my sheerest armor   my filly signal   just one sign of
the <u>fearless core</u> you do not want to mess wit   my strength is night-black
is island-rock   is hard but alive as coral reef   the lace

[handwritten: perpetual cycle of harassment]

the caribbean sea makes   no surprise <u>i'm *so hard eh*   *chains and*</u>
<u>*whips excite me*</u>   i love leather   i will strut
the red carpet in any city in the world   in necklines down
to there   shorts rising up to here   but i'm the
<u>barbadian mirage</u>   the weed-hungry boys in the back alleys and busy streets
of the world   dem cah look but never touch   i'm dizzy with

[handwritten: stereotypes]

power   but rubber-muscled from the weight of the role i model   mi paint
mi politics pon mi lips for de <u>young girls to read</u>   slip on
<u>courage like stilettos</u>   and in return   fair-weather fans bring roses to my
door   real love brings an <u>umbrella</u>   shelter for my only human face

legend

fern wept, let her eyes
    wet her tresses, her cheeks,
        her feet. the cheerlessness

    rendered her blessed,
strengthened her nerve.
    even then, she'd seen

        she needed her regrets
    melted. the weep-fest
helped her shed her tender

    edges, she felt the steel
        emerge. she'd served her
    sentence. she'd get herself

west, persevere, exert
    herself. they'd tell bess—
        her sweet bess!—fern'd

    deserted her. bess knew
better! when she left, fern
    pretended phlegm, yet

        she'd pledged she'd never
    rest ere she freed bess:
the excellent secret they

kept between themselves.
when fern'd netted the
needed green, she'd send

bess her debt fee—then,
pressed, they'd sell her . . .
her self. (senseless!) *see,*

bess, she'd greet her when
they re-met, necks nestled,
flesh welded, essence-deep,

we knew we'd effect the deed!
we're the bees knees! they'll
never see cleverer femmes.

legit-i-mate

legal measures gave us the rule of thumb.

antebellum legislation made a clean sweep

of lawful unions in certain quarters. some men

accumulate wives religiously, a practice which

frequently goes unstated. government outlawed

loving in virginia. a president once proclaimed,

ask not what your relationship can do for your country—

there's no telling. the marriages with the most

sanctity immigrate to the homeland with the most

security. *dear john, your proposition ate my california*

marriage license, so my honest woman can't make

an honest woman of me. fair trade act: the government

stays out of our bedrooms, and in exchange

~~our bedrooms stay out of the tax code.~~

there's been a separation of church and state,

but perhaps it's time for a formal divorce.

improphised

    [1] imagine peter, not nodding
over his palms that dawn,
but praying the vindictive

    [2] prayers of the righteous,
drawing enough testosterone
up from his balls to light

    [3] all the dew in the garden
afire, more than enough
to keep him awake, enough

    [4] even to make him slap
judas's silvery lips before
they could kiss the sacrifice,

    [5] causing chaos among the spear-
bearing romans : imagine
him alive with the fury

    [6] of love and utterly blind
to the lacerated look on his
friend-of-friends' face, denying

    [7] nothing, not his name, not
his faith, not his rage, hurling
affirmations at his inquisitors—

[8] *yes, i am the man!* : this peter,
all flesh and flood, imagine
him murderously steadfast,

[9] less rock than stone, a self-
made weapon, still weeping
at the cock's crow, every pre-

[10] diction re-writing itself anew
in his woeful image : human if
he did and human if he didn't.

cogito ergo loquor

some brutalities are unspeakable, and we shouldn't
force ourselves to speak of them.

—ching-in chen

i think, therefore i am.

—rené descartes

i.

i could speak of the economic fist that slammed
    into the body of the elderly woman downstairs ::
used to be downstairs : taking her time but not
    taking help bringing in the groceries : lucky to
live in a first-floor apartment :: less lucky now :
    she learned how many more dollars a month
above her rent the building owners need to turn
    ~~a trick~~ a profit :: did they foresee how many
slow steps she'd take to find a new home ? did
    they bruise their tight red knuckles ?: the grey
powdering the half-nappy pony-puff she pulled
    her hair into bought her a little time but what
will it get her on the open market ?: her eviction
    was the fourth bomb dropped this month in
the war on poverty the wealthy are waging on my
    block : in which i am a diplomat and a survivor.

ii.

to speak of fists is not to speak of fistulas : false
    cognates we might misrecognize as kin :: the

latter comes from latin and a word meaning *pipe*
    or *tube* but the one does not lead necessarily
to the other :: as anarcha's doctor taught us : right
    after swearing the hypocritic oath : fistulas are
torn tissue : as in : a passage between the urethra
    and the vagina :: as one cannot close the vulva at
will this causes : in terms of plumbing : a leak ::
    i do not mention this to be vulgar : *vulgar* and
vulva being another case of fake cousins kissing
    :: anarcha's condition resulted from slave labor :
the difficult delivery of a tiny new hand unto its
    master :: o there are other causes : ask the war-
weary women of the congo :: but upon advice
    and consideration i will not speak of them.

iii.

nor should we force ourselves to be silent ::
    unmentionables once were underwear : where
were the worst brutalities then ?: buried under
    under in the most vulnerable organs and held
down by that busy muscle the tongue :: in
    silence *unspeakable* becomes *unthinkable* : a word
like *numberless* that runs *can't* into *won't* :: some
    unthinkable things i just keep thinking about :
a 7-year-old girl and a gang rape facilitated by
    her 15-year-old sister for money : a 95-year-old
floridian woman stripped of her wet diaper
    by airport security : a congolese man who wears
pads meant for menstrual blood after years as
    a prisoner of war : companies seeking off-shore-
drilling permits while uncontrollable oil is still
    ravaging an ecosystem :: thinkable : unthinkable.

iv.

perhaps *unimaginable* should stand between

   ourselves and the worst :: if i spare myself

and you : gentle reader : if i spare us the graphic

   details will we still write checks to fund the less

poetic work of others ?: or is *checks* itself too far

   from lyrical for your taste ?: palatable poetry

comes in fewer flavors than edible cuisine : yet

   taste and *palatable* swing between the tongue

and the mind : a dance this poem has already

   performed :: can we empathize without taking

on the trauma ?: can we pursue cognition by

   a path that cuts through the body but bypasses

the gut ?: i must insist that my need for shelter :

   clean air & water : dignity : good food : security

: love : peace : and joy exists in you and every

   you : us : humans :: we are not false cognates.

philosophically immune

can i deduce the nature of humanity from the relationship of american and multinational pharmaceutical corporations to african women with hiv? ~ is it natural to test pharmaceuticals on people who are citizens of less powerful nations, members of a devalued gender, representatives of a maligned race? ~ is it logical? ~ is it cost-effective? ~ is the nature of the relationship of american and multinational pharmaceutical corporations to african women with hiv economic or human? ~ economic or humane? ~ are african women with hiv human? ~ are african women human? ~ are africans human? ~ are american and multinational pharmaceutical corporations human? ~ are american corporations human? ~ are americans human? ~ are american corporations citizens? ~ are africans american? ~ are african americans multinational? ~ can humans have a relationship to american and multinational pharmaceutical corporations? ~ are corporations corporeal? ~ are corporations real? ~ are corporations corpses? ~ are corporations gendered? ~ are women representative? ~ are humans incorporated? ~ are humans pharmaceutical? ~ is hiv pharmaceutical? ~ is nature pharmaceutical? ~ is nature humane? ~ is nature natural? ~ are nations natural? ~ are nations raced? ~ are nations corporations? ~ are nations cost-effective? ~ is nationality a test? ~ can i deduce the humanity of the reader from the relationship of the reader to american and multinational pharmaceutical corporations? ~ can i deduce the nature of the reader from the relationship of the reader to african women with hiv?

"the people want the regime to fall"

march, too, this year was nervy, making all
it could of winter's costume, flaunting snow
and sleet, slapping our stiffening cheeks cold
        and red, wearing white well past when it's called
        for, leaving the tree limbs smooth, the buds stalled
deep in their dreams, a too-static tableau,
everything with liquid in its veins so
        damn-near frozen, spring slowed down to a crawl.

still, hope springs, we drink in every season,
and people take root, sprout, and blossom in
the capitol greens and the public squares
        in cities near and far. call it treason,
        if you will. i call it nature, human,
to forge an april from the heat of our desires.

a dark scrawl

war can't amass a brass tack. war's
all bad acts and lack, scandal

    and graft. watch flags clash and tanks

attack camps. arms crack — rat-a-
tat-tat! — and ban calm. cabals

    plan vast land grabs and trash far-

away clans' shacks, pads, plants, halls,
and farms. war's fans track maps that

    warp and adapt as rash hands

grasp at lands that attract. rag-
clad lads and gals gnaw small snacks,

    catch-as-catch-can. war's gray days

last and last and, as man slays
man and clans fall apart, can

    wax halfway banal. ask: what

attar can mask war's stank past?
what fragrant balm allay all

qualms and angst war spawns? alas,

sad mamas bawl, what wan dawn
shall mark war's last gasp? what art,

pray, shall patch tracts war ransacks,

mass and spark lads' and gals' war-
raw shards, and call glad days back?

a one-act play

a man in blue sees the black in man, sees the black boy as man, sees the black man as bear, bears the black bear ill will, makes the black man ill, sees the black man on the make, seizes upon the man's black make-up, makes up what he will(s). the black man sees the man in blue, be's the blues in man, demands the blues back (off), deems the blues black, does the blues deed, deeds the blues back, lacks what blacks need, needs the true blue, bleeds the true black. blue and black: z'that a fact? black and blue: re-do. re-do.

fukushima blues

i've
long
heard
tokyo
calling

wanted
to
see
japan
someday

long
time
tokyo's
been
calling
my
name

come
see
japan
someday

well
i
thought
it
was
too
great
a
distance

now
i
see
japan
is
right
around
the
way

i
didn't
feel
the
earthquake

that
tsunami
wave
didn't
even
touch
my
toes

i
never
felt
the
earth's
super
shimmy

and
her
tsunami
wave
didn't
get
nowhere
near
my
toes

but
the
aftershocks
are
still
quiet-
coming

and
i'm
drowning
in
them,
lord
knows

i've
long
heard
tokyo
calling

a
distant
voice
from
a
distant
shore

so
long
i've
heard
tokyo
calling

but
never
made
it
to
that
distant
shore

so
the
earthquake
shook
loose
a
piece

and
the
tsunami
dragged
it
right
up
to
my
door

the
quake
shut
down
the
fukushima
party

and
the
tsunami
took
out
the
trash

the
quake
shut
down
fukushima
the
hard
way

and
the
tsunami
took
care
of
the
trash

i'm
not
sure
where
all
the
junk
got
dumped

but
i
heard
that
it
made
quite
a
splash

a
ghost
ship
sailed
itself
over
here

surrounded
by
all
kinds
of
debris

a
crewless
ship
haunted
its
way
across
the
pacific

along
with
autos,
unmarked
barrels,
and
all
kind
of
debris

shit's
washing
up
all
along
the
left
coast

loud
with
high-
volume
radio-
activity

i remember when i was scared to try sushi

but once i did i was hooked

yeah i used to be squeamish about sushi

but the first bite got me hooked

now i'm an asian fusion junkie

but i don't want the tuna in my sushi cooked

we laid a little egg of cesium-137

on hiroshima in 1945

we laid another egg of cesium-137— a fat one—

on nagasaki back in '45

boy, those eggs hatched like they were supposed to

and, man oh man, has the species multiplied . . .

jim crow stole my father's wings

that cat was a straight arrow, flying like he'd been shot
true from a sturdy bow, in a steady parallel to earth. scot

free : his tail all feathers, his high all feet. he kept a cloud
in his pocket, the wind's whistle between his teeth. proud

of his hours, his ratings, his license to skill, he took off
after a uniform and a jet. but a foul thing, packing a roof

and crawling in his wake, fused its (b)lack to his (f)light :
an arbitrary shadow screwed to his heels, waited his float

with gross ballast, dragged him down when gravity'd failed.
he held on to the whistle, sent it soaring up from the soil.

—after eduardo corral

supply and demand

(handwritten: limited supply & demand)

the more black boys you have, the more you want. *(handwritten: incarceration system)*

you act like we're swimming in black boys. *(handwritten: or drowning)*

you can't keep black boys in your pocket.

if you had a million black boys, what would you do with them?

do you think we're made of black boys?

your black boys are all tied up in property.

black boys won't solve all your problems.

you don't just find black boys lying in the street.

it takes black boys to make black boys.

most people don't know how to save black boys.

black boys don't grow on trees.

(handwritten annotations: "containment"; "reference back to the 'you'"; "terminology used in the news to reference black men"; "not naturally available, like air")

73

stop : meet with me here, weapons at rest,
on this stage of reciprocal dreaming : you
imagine you hear my desperate breathing :
and i, your eardrum, a small heart, beating

iv.

blues modality

What betrays revolution is the need
for revolution. It can not stop in life.
Whoever seeks to freeze the moment is

instantly, & for that instant, mad!

—amiri baraka

preface to a twenty-first-century

survival guide

lately, green has smacked
of disgruntlement and black
looks askance on its assigned
roles, while all the blues
team up for the takeover.

pretty is as pretty does.

and now, my mornings fill
with coffee and bad news, the bad
news as finely ground as the beans
and sprinkled in like an antidote.

it's not just for breakfast anymore.

and then, when i thought my habits
could not be broken or even
hemmed, i smelled the smoke
coming off my overworked cells—
left ventricle, right ventricle—

the little engines that could.

    —after amiri baraka

senzo

—carnegie hall, october 19, 2014

beauty eludes me, usually. i soak
up the lush red, violet, indigo blooms
    abdullah ibrahim's cool fingers pluck
from the keyboard's bed, but bring to these 'rooms'

(stanzas forged from replayed past as today's
not-news) no solacing bouquets. my weeds?
    i conjure rough green to explode from seeds
so furious they bleed—or, grieving, raise

crab grass and blue notes, peppered with rust,
where he grows flowers. yes, i tend my plants
    incisively : no phrase that droops or wants
out of the sun survives long. but the rest

run wild, flush vivid, throw shade, deluge fruit,
lavishly express their dissonant root.

lotto motto

first thing, i'm gonna paint the toothbrush red. i'm gonna quit my jalopy. i'm gonna whip up a few dead horses and put them out to passion. i'm gonna wash up on some distant score. first thing, i'm gonna get the expel outta dodge. i'm gonna run like the wound. i'm gonna wash away our skins. i'm gonna blow this icicle point, first thing. first thing i'm gonna do, i'm gonna freeze dry my clown wig. i'm gonna stumble under your breath. yeah, i'm gonna make like elvis and exit the gilding. i'm gonna spit out that taste of punch, then wash my mouth out with hope. are you kidding me? first thing, i'm gonna hit the toad, i'm gonna get down to brass tracks, i'm gonna head for the thrills, if it's the last thing i do.

a one-act play

create a livable world. you'll need water. trees and air, a food supply. you may want cell phones, condominiums, social hierarchies, but they're optional. go ahead—take as many days as you like. it's just a play. when you're done, you undo it. be creative. go wild! it should be a hard act to follow.

to be continued blues

the old folks had it right: the darkness always
    plays with the light. happy curl of bessie's voice,

springing through *backwater blues*, strong pulled-tight
spiral riding the plane that rocks upon the pianist's
    knuckles. moonfaced, the proof and promise of sun

shining out of her skin. when her vocal lightning
    strikes, sorrow gleams and winks: the joke is on

tomorrow. forgotten knowledge leaks from r&b's
    rusty acronym. thought hip hop had leaped over

that lesson, but chuck d tucked it under a rhyme
    the old school had it right. our darkness always

shines out on its kin when it goes vocal. lightning-
fast lines link black butterflies to (who's that) blues
    ladies, or last trains leaving sundown towns to new

orleans' no-buses going no-where fast. sky's so
    dark and bright. she wailed 911 a long time ago.

of speech

they spoke with blue they
blued they gave us
the blues their presence was
bluing they blue us over
aside they spoke with metal with
their barricades they
barricaded they barred they
used bars to divide
the sidewalk they used
bars to divide us
from other people they barred
us in a few bars of the blues

the barricades were
bare the barricades were
blue they spoke with
badge they spoke with badger they
spoke with loudspeakers
that spoke louder
than the speakers at our rally we
rallied we spoke together we
spoke louder than the loudspeakers
we spoke over
the blues we spoke of the blues

they spoke with laws they
spoke of laws they spoke

of enforcement they
spoke of force they meant
force they meant us to be in
force in their force they
are force they are in forces their
forces spoke with loudspeakers
their forces blue us away
with the force of their speech they
drowned us in their blue speech

they spoke of arrest they
did not arrest our
attention we spoke of freedom
we spoke of speech we spoke
of browns and blacks they
spoke with numbers we
spoke with numbers we spoke
of numbers we numbered
their crimes we have
their number their blues
number their days are
numbered our days are numbered

they spoke with blue with
barricade with badge
with authority but not with
impunity their bullets speak
with impunity they
speak with handcuffs their
speech is handcuffed their speech

is not free their unfreedom
of speech is/blue their blacks
speak blue their browns speak
blue their whites speak blue

we   have the freedom of speech
we used the freedom   of speech to speak
of freedom loudly we   spoke freedom
loudly and in   that place and
in that speaking we lived and did not die
we spoke and   did not die we
spoke freedom and   nothing happened
except   this poem this freedom we
spoke with freedom and   our speech
of freedom spoke   louder than
blues than badges our   speech of
freedom spoke over their   loudspeakers
our freedom spoke   over their barricades
and onto this page   ¡yes!   one freedom

                                    led to another

                    —millions march rally, columbus circle,
                            nyc, july 17, 2015, one year after
                                    the murder of eric garner

the obsolete army

the obsolete army works with bayonets and horses
    the bayonets they dismantle for parts
    the horses they groom and set free in the newly opened pastures

the obsolete army has time on their wrists
    they take active duty in 8-hour shifts
    their watches are timepieces—they aren't on guard

the obsolete army exercises every day
    they push-up the people who are closest to their dreams
    they pull-up those just getting off the ground

the obsolete army debates the value of war museums
    they know an unlocked world is the key to freedom
    they know how close memorial is to mourning

the obsolete army is increasingly multi-lingual
    comment dit-on en français: *arabic is spoken here*
    when they say *tanks*, they're practicing their patois

the obsolete army understands nostalgia
    they welcome the obsolete patriots carrying protest signs
    they provide tea, coffee, and athletic competitions

the obsolete army is open 24/7
    the privates promote the general welfare of the publics
    you enter it yourself when you're most at peace

the obsolete army repurposes the obsolete words

they donate _collateral damage_ to the financial industry

they apply _infantry_ to the maternity wards' ever-renewing ranks

truth in advertising

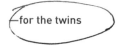 for the twins

little girls™

"sugar 'n spice 'n everything nice"

nutrition facts

serving size **1 girl** (2 years old)
servings per container **2**

amount per serving	rec'd daily allowance
sugar 25g	90%
spice 759g	98%
everything nice 5mg	27%
everything else 363kg	200%

ingredients: wood (hard-headed), sponge (absorbing juice and juicy words), rubber (bouncing off each other), sand (getting into everything), sulfur (loud-smelling and -sounding), hydrogen (self-igniting fuel), helium (lifting pitch and spirits), plastic (surprisingly durable), oil (in your grasp), lead (at rest in your arms), glass (transparent), elastic (forgiving), magnets (attracting attention), time (repeating reoccurring re-cycling), smoke (fire), rain (scattered thunderstorms), wind (rushing through).

everything nice is the least

The words in parenthesis are neg while the words outside the parentheses are everday objects, almost as if you are trying to hide these "negative" aspects

upon this plot

—with a line from nourbese philip

while it is still wet

    etched with now: *august 1965*

drag time through concrete
on the tip of a stick

a time of ownership, property

    erect with new: the baby rushing
                                into the home
          prepared for her
                  (november   and leaves
                           and stays

at the foot of the garage
the driveway laid: flat monument
                     to a family   history

a house built for   2   5   4

on the corner of ph.d. in zoology   (dr. hubert b. CROUCH   drive
        and painter of quilts   (faith RINGGOLD   drive

young sisters pretend   with black & blonde baby dolls & barbies
    to do almost anything

HAYNES MANOR

a lofty name holding a bit of black nashville aloft

a community of educators, entrepreneurs, office workers &
    government employees

a neighborhood built for black families on the MOORMANS ARM
    (not a fleeing swan's wing

a couple hundred brown acres to green with lawns from seed,
    young maples & sycamores maturing

at every intersection, possibility:

BONTEMPS	(arna	novelist, poet)
WORK	(john wesley	composer)
ROWAN	(carl	journalist)
DUNBAR	(paul laurence	poet)
REVELS	(hiram rhodes	u.s. senator)
DUBOIS	(w. e. b.	editor, intellectual)
BALDWIN	(james	essayist, novelist)
AUGUSTA	savage)	sculptor)

(won't let a _surname hold us back_ . . .

there, 3 generations of children
    biking   pumping uphill earns the return, frees the breeze
     jumping rope
      running   barefoot on the glittering asphalt, spring grass
       playing kickball   forcing the cars to slow   driveway's home
        waiting on buses
         chasing dogs   yelling down the block
          listening to radios   looked out for
         growing up   almost safe
        (knowing or not knowing they lived

on streets named for   WHO WE ARE
                and   WHO WE HOPE YOU'LL BE

and from that corner house
at the bottom of the hill

        edged with knew: the poet rushing
                                             into the world

                    prepared

how long has this jayne been gone?

-

not long   not long

in fact
    she's back

flapping with the gale force laughter of the first kites of march
growling like a motorcycle of liberation
howling like the angel of field hollers at the bleachers of poetic apathy
    where they're always ready to make some noise but never get in the game

o yes, she's back
back like she was never gone

still blueswashing over the whitewashing of the music
still pinning the tale on the covert donkey of domination
still hissing wisdom into the imperial bathwater
still cussing the fuck out of evil rapist punks
    (and the friendly ones too)

she's right beneath your mama's left breast
right up in the cook-footed cornbread
still breaking out like sweat on the drummer's forehead
still chuckling in the backyard over her hot diaspora stew

can't you hear her?
rumbling like an earthquake through the crowded blocks of watts
sizzling like the wind off the ancient coast of senegal
honking like the traffic symphony in the hot-sauce streets of new york
crashing onto the untamed sands of the people's beaches of cuba

how long has this jayne, this breathtaking jayne cortez been gone?

not long   not long

in fact
     she's back

yeah, back for seconds
a little more armstrong funk in the sunshine
another helping of that spicy césairean calalou
     with a bit of red pepper poet mixed in
another round of big mama thornton blues brew— right, humblebee?

yeah, she's looking for a second slice of that wicked shit guillén cooked up
another bite of that african truth casserole chano pozo's serving from his conga—
     very fine, very fine
one more taste of the scatology spittle ella's still slinging round the savoy ballroom
one more ride on the trane this side of time, before she takes it to her final destination

have you seen her?
drinking the conjure woman's pot likker straight out of the pot
sashaying across the evening sky like a bouquet of blackgirls' smiles

have you heard her?
talk-singing her gut-bucket lullabies into the ears of desperate children,
     exhausted men, and outraged women
sweeping the dust of corporate-sponsored exploitation off the bandstand
     with her fire-spitting lyrical jazz clean-up crew

have you felt her?
rattling your bones with the daily news of the latest pro-democracy drone strike

licking with sandpaper-cat-tongue kisses the numbed shell
    of cultural desensitization to violence we call 'paying the bills'

have you seen her?
have you seen her?

how long how long has our jayne been gone?

not long   not long

she's no farther away than the sound of her name and her hellified poetry
    ringing out of our long-memoried throats

if we act right
    she'll be right back

du bois in ghana

at 93, you determined to pick up and go—
and *stay* gone. the job nkrumah called you to,
to create, at last, your *encyclopedia africana*
    (encompassing a continent chipped

like wood beneath an axe, a large enough
diaspora to girdle the globe, and a mere four
thousand years) was either well-deserved
    sinecure or well-earned trust

that your health was as indestructible as
your will. my mind wrestles with possible pictures:
the victorian sensibility, the charcoal wool
    formality of your coats and vests, the trim

of your beard as sharp as the crease of your
collar—how would these du boisian essentials
hold up to sub-saharan heat? would
    your critical faculties wilt in accra's

urban tropics as i've read that westerners'
are wont to do? dr. du bois, i presume
you took the climate in stride, took to it,
    looked out your library's louvered windows

onto a land you needed
neither to condemn nor conquer,
and let the sun tell you what you already knew:
    this was not a port to pass on.

your 95th birthday photo found you bathed
in white cloth, cane still in hand, sharing a smile
with a head of state who knew your worth—joy
        that this nation's birth occurred in time

for you to step out of a cold, cold storm
into outstretched arms. would your pan-
african dream have survived a dictatorial
        nkrumah, an nkrumah in exile? you took

the prerogative of age and died without telling,
without knowing. a half-century later, here
in the country where you were born, i look
        into a screen and watch as, near and far, a pan-

demic of violence and abuse staggers the planet.
we seed the world with blood, grow
bleeding, harvest death and the promise
        of more. when i turn bitter, seeing no potential

for escape, i think of the outrages you saw—wars,
lynchings, genocide, mccarthy, communism's
failure to rise above corrupting power
        any better than capitalism had, the civil rights

movement's endless struggle—and how
you kept writing and walking, looking
for what you knew was out there. your memory,
        your tireless radiant energy, calls me

to my work, to my feet, insisting
that somewhere on the earth, freedom is
learning to walk, trying not to fall,
    and, somewhere, laboring to be born.

cosmography

—after jay wright

a call opera'd me open, dusty
evidence : we breathe light, particulate,
consumed, consuming : aria—easy,
but true : i heard it, watched it command,
cajole, rolling bright echoes of distance,
motes, notes, dancing illumination in
and out on my individual wind

circe / odysseus / black odysseys (a remix-collage)

—for romare bearden and nina simone

i am black, but sorcerous   i mean trouble   gonna
put long uneasy miles between me and my home, but it's not
a one-way ticket   this here's *circe's domain*—come on in and set a
spell   hey, wanderer   the north's no escape, just another stop
on some lonesome railroad line   listen: rejection's telling
you to improvise   *little girl blue*   cotton-blue   i do you this way,

      cause i can   you bring your beast to my door,
      you're asking for trouble   look: when i tell it, *the odyssey* is
      mine   if the gods spew at you their red-eyed fury,

you might not ever find home   harlem swings me a little
better   philadelphia loves me some, brother   carolina won't
stop me from shadowing my passion   pierce me with your *other* spear—
the one that won't leave me bleeding   you and me, we can pursue
things under these wide blue skies that will surely make
you forget about home   i got the sea chasing me   what can i
do but keep moving   barbados   aeaea   st. maarten

      i follow the blue-black keys where they lead   *bc-bach!*   o you
      ain't seen the full power of my mojo, baby   who's
      lying to who   believe me: my wand doubles as a sword

i swear: my voice is honey and venom   picture ithaca   i assemble
love from cut-up color, canvas and glue   daddy, if a year is all
you got to give, give it here   forever's a big blue illusion
anyhow   see all the skulls   marriage won't outlast freedom

and liberia ain't the same as liberty   tell me, how can
i trust a woman with a snake for a bracelet   well, it
don't mean a thing, if it ain't got that sting   why should i
care about penelope if you don't   if yellow   if red   if orange
if green   if blue   it's true: i'm dying to hear *the sirens' song*
you shape your future from your past   the geometry of
don't can be transformed   troubled women walking   i
want *to bring forth a people*   an outrageous magic shakes
me   *everybody knows about mississippi*   many men destroyed

i'm blue, but i won't be blue always   never forget my pillow is
yours   red sun shining against a full moon—night-noon's a sign,
right   aix marks the spot   one last stab at some kind of home
now go   get back out there and <u>do what you were born to</u> do

notes

Epigraphs to the book are from: Fred Moten's *In the Break*, Sonia Sanchez's "An Anthem (for the ANC and Brandywine Peace Community)," and Toni Cade Bambara's "An Interview with Toni Cade Bambara" (by Kay Bonetti).

that's a rap (sheet music for alphabet street): If you don't know Prince's cut "Alphabet Street," then you can't hear the last line of the poem the way I do. This should be all the excuse you need to get *Lovesexy* (1988). {Prince, U R Forever in My Life.}

The epigraph to section i is from Erica Hunt's "The Mood Librarian."

the way we live now :: was written shortly after the murders at the Emanuel AME Church of Charleston, South Carolina (June 17, 2015).

buried truths: The stanzas of this poem take their syntax from lines in Keorapetse Kgositsile's "When Brown Is Black," whose opening stanza begins: "Are you not the light / that does not flicker / when murderers threaten summertime / passions of our time . . . "

banking on amnesia: It seems the national amnesia is already catching up with the relatively recent events that inspired this poem—collectively known as the Occupy Movement—as well as the much earlier issues the poem references. For the record, the poem is not a critique of that movement, but a wish, in solidarity with American Indians/Native Americans, that the language adopted as the movement's rallying cry had been more thoughtfully chosen.

in a no-win zone: This poem is written in the form called the "prisoner's constraint," which allows the poet to use only letters whose parts do not ascend above or descend below the basic horizon of the text.

corrective rape (or, i'm here to help): This poem was inspired in part by the violent crimes terrorizing black lesbians in South Africa: "According to a report by international group ActionAid, 10 new cases of lesbians being raped are reported every week in Cape Town alone."—Paula Brooks, for *LezGetReal*, April 4, 2010. The rapists' oxymoronic term for their crimes suggested to me a continuum (though not an equivalence) between this violence and certain kinds of "elective" violence women are persuaded to undergo.

Sex Trafficking Incidents in the Life of a Slave Girl in the USA (or, The Nation's Plague in Plain Sight): All non-italicized text in this poem is excerpted from Chapter X of *Incidents in the Life of a Slave Girl*, by Harriet Jacobs; all italicized text is excerpted from "Sex Trafficking in the USA," by Yamiche Alcindor, *USA Today*, September 27, 2012.

The epigraph to section ii is from Thylias Moss's "Interpretation of a Poem by Frost." Her stunning performance of this poem at AWP 2015 will be with me forever.

topsy's notes on taxonomy: This poem was inspired in part by the work of Caribbean philosopher Sylvia Wynter, as taken up by Alexander Weheliye in his book *Habeas Viscus: Racializing Assemblages, Biopolitics, and Black Feminist Theories of the Human*. He writes: "Following Sylvia Wynter, I use Man to designate the modern, secular, and western version of the human that differentiates full humans from not-quite-humans and nonhumans on the basis of biology and economics."

from topsy in wonderland: This poem finds Topsy—whom I've rescued from *Uncle Tom's Cabin*—in a somewhat different world, suggested by Lewis Carroll's classic books, *Alice's Adventures in Wonderland* and *Through the Looking-Glass and What Alice Found There*. Citations are to chapters of these texts—as well as to the full record of *Topsy's Adventures*, of course—for those interested in comparisons. To my delight, I discovered recently that Alison Saar had been dreaming of Topsy's release as well. Her vision accompanies mine here.

The epigraph to section iii is from Gwendolyn Brooks's "A Bronzeville Mother Loiters in Mississippi. Meanwhile, a Mississippi Mother Burns Bacon."

a-lyrical ballad (or, how america reminds us of the value of family) joins the tradition of elegies for unjustly slain black people in the United States, which includes such works as Douglas Kearney's "Tallahatchie Lullaby, Baby," many sections of Claudia Rankine's *Citizen*, Marilyn Nelson's *A Wreath for Emmett Till*, and Gwendolyn Brooks's "A Bronzeville Mother Loiters in Mississippi. Meanwhile, a Mississippi Mother Burns Bacon" and "The Last Quatrain of the Ballad of Emmett Till," along with many others. The main title nods at William Wordsworth. The poem is dedicated to Emmett Till, Sandra Bland, Amadou Diallo, Renisha McBride, Trayvon Martin, Rekia Boyd, Tamir Rice, and . . . .

keep your eye on riffs on many things, beginning with "John Brown's Ford," a children's activity-song revision of the folk song "John Brown's Body"; toward the end, the poem borrows one line intact from Mark Twain's parody of the "Battle Hymn of the Republic." These songs all share the same melody.

song in the back yard is in a form Terrance Hayes invented and dubbed the "golden shovel." Italicized lines are titles and fragments from Rihanna's oeuvre and interviews, except one: "*my love is too // complicated to have thrown back in my face*" is from the incomparable Ntozake Shange's *for colored girls who have considered suicide / when the rainbow is enuf.* This poem needed her.

"*the people want the regime to fall*": The "year" referenced in the poem was 2012, when pro-union workers held extended protests at the Wisconsin State Capitol.

The epigraph to section iv is from Amiri Baraka's "'There Was Something I Wanted to Tell You.' (33) Why?"

senzo: The title of this poem, also the title of one of Ibrahim's fairly recent albums, means "ancestor" in both Chinese and Japanese, and "creator" in the Sotho language spoken by his father (according to Ibrahim's website).

upon this plot borrows and takes inspiration from a short fragment ("erect with new") in M. NourbeSe Philip's breathtaking poem "She Tries Her Tongue, Her Silence Softly Breaks." I take off from her phrase in quite a different direction than she goes, and I heartily recommend that you read it in its original context, where it does its best work.

how long has this jayne been gone? : We call your name, Jayne Cortez (1934–2012).

circe / odysseus / black odysseys (a remix-collage): This poem incorporates or paraphrases titles and lyrics (italicized), process notes, and biographical details from the work and lives of Romare Bearden and Nina Simone—and draws as well on *The Odyssey*.

acknowledgments

I am grateful to the editors of these journals and anthologies for the initial opportunity to share some of the poems herein (sometimes in earlier versions) with a reading audience:

The Account: A Journal of Poetry, Prose, and Thought—"in the california mountains, far from shelby / county, alabama and even farther from / the supreme court building, the black poet / seeks the low-down from a kindred entity"

Bearden's Odyssey: Poets Respond to the Art of Romare Bearden—"circe / odysseus / black odysseys (a remix-collage)"

The Black Scholar—"how long has this jayne been gone?"

BOMBlog—"the obsolete army"

Bone Bouquet—"if a junco" and "sore score"

Boston Review—"lotto motto"

boundary 2—"that's a rap (sheet music for alphabet street)" and "keep your eye on"

CURA: A Literary Magazine of Art & Action—"cogito ergo loquor"

esque—"banking on amnesia" and "corrective rape (or, i'm here to help)"

Feminist Formations—"philosophically immune," "legit-i-mate," and "Sex Trafficking Incidents in the Life of a Slave Girl in the USA (or, The Nation's Plague in Plain Sight)"

FENCE—"legend" and "fukushima blues"

The Golden Shovel Anthology: New Poems Honoring Gwendolyn Brooks—"song in the back yard"

Letters to the Future: Black Women's Experimental Poetry—"topsy talks about her role" and "from *topsy in wonderland*"

Literary Hub—"topsy's notes on taxonomy"

The Nation—"improphised"

Nevermore and the Living Poetry Project—["stop : meet with me here . . ."]

Obsidian—"upon this plot"

pluck! The Journal of Affrilachian Arts & Culture (Black Poets Speak Out special issue)—"supply and demand" and "buried truths"

POEM (UK)—"acrobatic"

Poem-a-Day (Academy of American Poets)—"du bois in ghana," "mirror and canvas,"
and "playing with fire"

Poetry—"senzo"

The Poetry Bus (UK)—"truth in advertising"

Poetry Salzburg—"weather or not"

Public Pool—"to be continued blues"

qarrtsiluni—"in a no-win zone"

Tin House—"i declare war" and "a dark scrawl"

Torch Literary Arts—"what's not to liken?"

Tri-Quarterly—"'the people want the regime to fall'"

Tuesday; An Art Project—"the way we live now ::"

The Volta Book of Poems—"studies in antebellum literature (or, topsy-turvy)"

Written Here: The Community of Writers Poetry Review 2015—"haibun for a parasitic pre-
apocalyptic blues"

I would also like to thank the editors of these publications for reprinting these pieces:

The Best American Experimental Writing 2015—"fukushima blues"

The Best American Poetry 2015—"legend"

Black Gold: An Anthology of Black Poetry—"how long has this jayne been gone?" and
"philosophically immune"

Letters to the Future: Black Women's Experimental Poetry—"philosophically immune" and
"what's not to liken?"

POEM (UK)—"a dark scrawl"

Poem-a-Day: 365 Poems for Every Occasion—"playing with fire"

The Volta Book of Poems—"a dark scrawl," "legit-i-mate," "'the people want the regime to
fall,'" and "weather or not"

Women Write Resistance: Poets Resist Gender Violence—"corrective rape (or, i'm here to
help)"

With these obvious and already more or less public debts acknowledged, there remains the happy task of thanking a whole host of people whose time, energy, brilliant feedback, and generosity of all kinds are the *sine qua non* of this collection, which was a good five years in the making.

Let me begin with grateful thanks to Suzanna Tamminen, Stephanie Elliott Prieto, Jackie Wilson, Peter Fong, and everyone with Wesleyan and UPNE who embraced, designed, and shepherded this book; I am so lucky to have such an amazing publisher.

My gratitude for the ongoing blessing that is Cave Canem—alla y'all—a steady current of electricity humming in my literary life.

I really appreciate the wonderful poets and arts administrators who invited me to give readings in their communities during the years that I was writing this book. The opportunity to see and hear audiences respond to new-ish work has been incredibly helpful, as has the provocation to write something new that each reading constitutes.

Thank-yous to the wonderful poets I worked with in 2013 and 2015 at the Community of Writers Poetry Workshop in (as Sharon Olds lovingly calls it) Squawk! Valley, California, where several of these poems were drafted or inspired.

I am grateful to the Millay Colony of the Arts, where this manuscript got its start—especially director Caroline Crumpacker, occasional writing partner Cathy Wagner, and all the terrific artists who helped make "Edna's place" such a generative space.

Heartfelt thank-yous to Robin Kelley and Naomi Wallace for enabling me to see the ways my work circulates in an important new light.

Love to my parents and all of my family in Ohio and Georgia for saying the nicest things and letting me off the hook whenever poetry called.

Sincere appreciation to these dazzling writers who read a draft here and a draft there, or offered invaluable post-reading responses that enabled crucial revisions: Ross Gay, Meta DuEwa Jones, Krystal Languell, and Mendi Obadike.

For reading the whole manuscript and giving me honest comments that saved this book from all manner of mistakes and infelicities, my thanks to: Brenda Coultas, Marcella Durand, Jennifer Firestone, Tracie Morris, and Karen Weiser.

For not only taking on the full manuscript and providing the necessary reality check on individual poems at times when I urgently needed to know what I'd written, but also being down for essential, intense, and energizing poetics conversations, my deep gratitude to Tonya Foster, Cathy Park Hong, and Douglas Kearney.

I owe a special debt of gratitude to the two formerly anonymous readers who reviewed the manuscript for Wesleyan and shed such generous light on the manuscript's flaws and strengths: Erica Hunt and Fred Moten. *Merci mille fois.*

I can never offer enough thanks to Alison Saar for sharing in my enthusiasm for a Topsy beyond Harriet Beecher Stowe's imaginative limits, and for gorgeously rendering this spirited young trickster at the crossroads of our interests in her. I'm thrilled to have Alison's permission to include her images in this volume.

And to Stéphane Robolin—who has read and re-read everything in this book multiple times; whose insights and questions so frequently opened the poems up for greater nuance or depth; and whose encouragement and belief never allowed me to doubt for long that this collection would finally be fully realized—the best and biggest part of my heart.

evie shockley is the author of several collections of poetry including *a half-red sea* (2006) and *the new black* (Wesleyan, 2011). She has won the Hurston/Wright Legacy Award in Poetry, the Holmes National Poetry Prize, the Stephen Henderson Award, and fellowships from Cave Canem, the Millay Colony for the Arts, the American Council of Learned Societies, and the Schomburg Center for Research in Black Culture of the New York Public Library. She currently is an associate professor of English at Rutgers University–New Brunswick and lives in Jersey City, New Jersey.